A children's story published by Stone Hedge Graphics, Inc.

www.stonehedgebooks.com
Phone: 262-692-6314

Book cover and text designed by Stone Hedge Graphics, Inc.

"Tinker's Tale"
First Edition

Betty Zak is a pen name used by the author

ISBN 978-0692453186

Printed in the United States of America

Tinker's Tale

The little creatures of earth
that fill our lives with love, joy,
and comfort, are a blessing to be
treasured. They will wholeheartedly
give their love and ask little in return.
All they desire is to be part
of a loving family, and hopefully
find a little boy or girl
to love them back.

This is the true story
of one of the blessings that came
my way, and changed my life
in a very wonderful way.

Once upon a time, on a still October night, a scruffy little creature ran on unsteady legs to the farthest corner of the room to hide from strangers that had come into her life for the first time that evening.

Other fluffy puppies, with tails wagging happily, jumped about with excitement in the hope that they would be picked up and cuddled by the friendly guests.

Then the air filled with a sound that the shy puppy hadn't expected as the guests said, *"All of these Yorkie puppies are really cute, but we came to see the West Highland Terrier."*

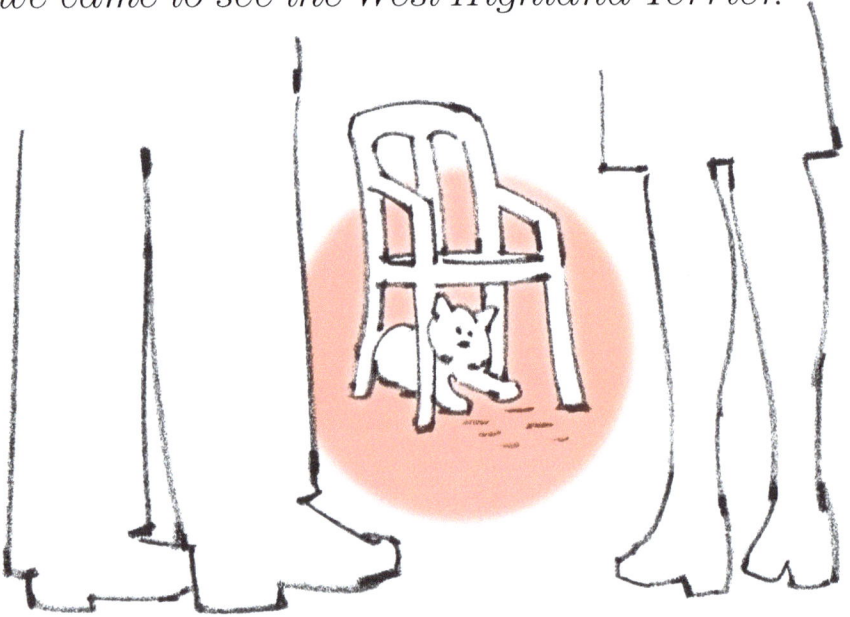

The room went quiet as the fuzzy puppy attempted to back up farther from view. It was no use. Within seconds she found herself being picked up by her breeder and carried back across the room; then she was gently placed in the soft warm hands of the person she would come to know as Betty.

At first the fuzzy little ball of fur shook nervously, then, feeling the caress of Betty's warm
hands and a gentle scratching across her scruffy
forehead she thought, *"Hey, this isn't so bad.
What was I so scared about? Who ever this
person is, she's very friendly!"*

The man with Betty looked at the puppy they had come to see and quietly whispered, *"She's as scruffy looking as a Brillo pad. I thought she would be soft and silky like the Yorkies. Are you sure you prefer her to the others?"*

Betty lifted the puppy up and held her close, looking at her tiny face. As Betty considered the man's comments, for the first time the scruffy fur ball found herself looking into Betty's eyes. The puppy tipped her head slightly as she stared back and thought to herself, *"Gee-whiz, she has pretty black eyes just like me!"*

4

While the Yorkies romped and jumped for attention Betty looked at the man and simply said, *"We came to see this little one. I feel her little heart pounding with excitement. I think she should come home with us."*

At that very moment the puppy extended her head and ever so gently licked Betty's nose. The puppy kiss would be the first of many-many kisses the two would share as they began their life together.

Lick!

The first night...

It was a long ride home with these strangers, but somehow the puppy felt wanted and very loved, so she simply curled up in Betty's lap and closed her eyes as the miles floated by.

Betty had prepared for her new friend's arrival with a soft puppy bed, several toys, a puppy dish, and the special food the puppy would need to grow strong and healthy. Upon entering her home Betty lowered the puppy to the floor. At first the puppy stood still not knowing what to make of her new surroundings. Then her fun-loving spirit kicked in, her tail wagged wildly, and she began running and sniffing in all of the rooms. As she ran across the plush carpet she stopped, turned over on her back, wiggling happily. *"Boy, I sure wish I could giggle,"* she *thought as she squirmed in the soft carpet.* *"What a cool place."*

Betty kept a close eye on her new friend to keep her from wandering too far while preparing her first puppy meal. Reaching down, Betty gave a small taste to the puppy, and then placed the rest in the puppy's bowl. From that moment the puppy never forgot where to find her food.

My name is…

That evening as the puppy sat on Betty's lap with the man the puppy would come to know as Zak sitting by their side. She could sense they were talking about her. Little did she know they were trying to come up with a name for her. As they watched a movie on television they saw the fairy Tinker Bell flying over the Disneyworld castle. *"That's it!" Betty said excitedly. "Let's call the puppy Tinker!"*

Zak looked at Betty, then at the scruffy little white ball looking up at him. *"Tinker? Tinker?"* He questioned. *"Well, she sure may have the magic to change our lives. Sure, Tinker it is!"*

The excited talk startled the puppy. She didn't understand what they were saying.

"Why are Betty and Zak looking into my eyes and repeating the same sound over and over. Tinker, Tinker, Tinker, they keep repeating while giving me a wonderful head scratching. If I'm going to get a nice head scratching every time I hear that sound I think I'm going to like that sound."

What does that sound mean?

Before long, whenever the puppy heard Betty make the sound *"Tinker"* she ran over to her to get her head lovingly scratched.

"What a cool idea," the puppy thought.

Oh, that's the spot!

Her other favorite sound came from Zak when he would say, *"Tinker, do you want rubber-downers?"* All Tinker knew when she heard that sound was that she would be treated to a great belly rub when she turned over. *"Oh boy,"* Tinker thought, *"great food, magical sounds like Tinker and rubber-downers, and a lot of kisses. I love this place."*

As the days went by Betty noticed that Tinker stayed very close to her wherever she would walk, whether in the house or outside. With Tinker always under foot, Betty began to realize that Tinker was trying to learn about the world around her. It was all very new to her, and she seemed to trust that Betty would take care of her.

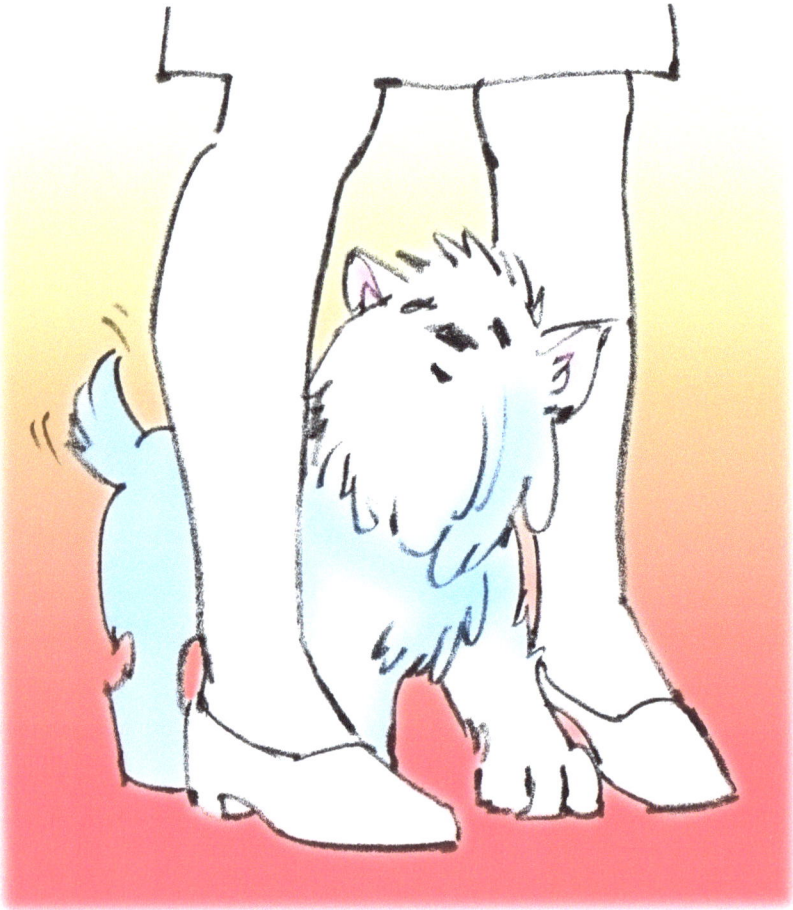

Lesson one...

One day, after her meal, the puppy ran about her new home exploring every corner. Suddenly she stopped, and with a funny look in her eyes, began to tinkle on the kitchen floor.

"Oh, oh," Betty thought. Lesson one was about to begin. Betty's finger wagged at the puppy, and it could tell that Betty's mood had changed somehow to being very unhappy. Tinker found herself being picked up and carried to the front door. Before long she stood outside on something soft and green, and Betty was making sounds of encouragement. *"What was she saying?"* the puppy thought. *"Oh well, I'll just sniff around in this cool green stuff a while. I kind of like the way it tickles my nose."*

After many trips to the cool green grass the puppy began to get the idea that Betty wanted her to tinkle outside. The clue was how Betty seemed so happy each time the puppy walked over to the door before she tinkled. Lesson one was a success.

Settling in...

Once Tinker understood her new world, off she would run in the fresh-cut green grass, rolling over every so often to wiggle in the fresh grass clippings. Other times she would showoff to Betty and Zak by running as fast as she could around and through the many evergreen trees in the yard until she plopped down with exhaustion, tail wagging and little pink tongue extended with what seemed to be a smiling face. Oh, how excited and happy she was during those bursts of fun.

Over time Tinker became very comfortable with sleeping with Betty and Zak in their bed. Zak made a stepladder next to the bed so that she could come and go as she pleased. She loved to snuggle up on top of the blankets and against Zak's leg as she dosed off. Then too, if she had to tinkle she would simply walk up to Zak's face and gently lick his cheek. That was Zak's signal to get up and follow her to the front door. Tinker was proud of the way she had trained Betty and Zak to do what she wanted them to do.

Then one day the world changed. Tinker went to the door as she always did, and Zak opened it. To her surprise her sweet-smelling green grass was nowhere to be seen. Instead, as far as she could see, it was all white. *"What is this stuff?"* she thought, as she carefully sniffed the air. Zak encouraged her to go out while saying *"snow Tinker, that's snow,"* so she slowly put her paw in the powdery white flakes. *"Wow, that's cold!"* she thought. Then she took another step, and another step. The powder came up to her belly as she plowed forward and finally tinkled. *"What happened to my beautiful green grass?"* she wondered. *"Where did it go?"*

Then her surprise turned to joy as she buried her nose in the snow and pushed through it like a plow. *"What fun!"* she thought to her self as she began to leap across the fresh snow creating a trail that only a happy puppy can make. She came to rest on all fours and looked back to be sure Zak was still with her. Then she took another leap into a small snowdrift and rolled over on her back making what could only be called a *puppy angel*. Her fresh green world had turned into a white wonderland, and she loved it.

Betty bought a beautiful red collar for Tinker with two silver tags dangling from it. One tag had Tinker's name on it and her address incase she was lost. The other had a little puppy on it and the words "Guardian Angel Protect Me." This was Tinker's first jewelry and she wasn't sure she liked the idea. As she walked through the house the tags would jingle. This was new to Tinker so she shook and shook to try to get the collar off at first. Finally she accepted the idea, trusting that Betty knew better.

As time went by Tinker became so fond of the collar that after her puppy baths she would run to Betty to have her put the collar back on. It was nice for Betty and Zak too. They could tell when Tinker was coming when they heard the tags jingling.

Bad puppy! Bad puppy!

A puppy knows when it is in trouble for something it shouldn't have done, like chewing the corner of a throw rug, or playing with the drapery cords until the drapery rods came crashing down. Tinker found such adventures fun until she heard the disapproving sound *"TINKER!!!"*

Oh, oh, it was time to run to her protective place under the dining room table. There, with six chairs tucked in around the table, she found that Betty and Zak had a hard time reaching her. When Zak removed a chair to retrieve Tinker she simply backed up further away from him.

But slowly the guilt got the best of Tinker. With her ears down and eyes drooped she rose and walked slowly over to Zak for her punishment, and licked his hand to show that she was sorry.

Zak looked at her sternly, then picked her up and gave her a gentle hug for giving him her gentle apology. Tinker knew that her world was a happy place once again when Betty began laughing at the way Zak and Tinker had looked as they crawled under the table.

A big girl now...

Tinker was growing fast. Her scruffy white puppy hair began to change to soft, silky white hair that sparkled silver in the sunlight. She seemed to know that she was beautiful. She was becoming a lady. With her changing to what might be called her teenage years she took on more responsibility for her surroundings. Although she loved to play in the house with her toys, if her toy would fall near any of Betty's decorations Tinker would stop, look at Betty, and wait for Betty to get the toy so Tinker wouldn't break anything. She was becoming a very smart little girl.

There were times when Tinker noticed that Betty and Zak had to go away. Those were the times she stayed at the neighbor's house. But it was always fun when at last Betty and Zak would appear at the door, because Tinker knew they would bring her a new toy. Betty would reach into her purse as Tinker stood in front of her with her tail wagging a hundred miles an hour with excitement. Once Betty said those magic words *"I've got a present for Tinker!"* she'd excitedly spin in a circle, then sit nervously. Betty slowly lowered the toy and Tinker would take it very carefully in her mouth. Then, without warning, she would run off excitedly whipping her toy around. Each time that happened she would be gone for several minutes to be alone with her new treasure; a reward for being a good girl while they were gone.

Another lesson learned...

Winter slowly turned to summer, and Tinker was looking forward to exploring outside once again. One summer day Tinker's leash became undone from the yard doggie-post as she detected a scent from the house next door. Even though she had the long leash still attached to her she ran toward the neighbor's house and slowly peaked into the open garage. Tinker decided to simply walk right in, dragging her leash behind her. Zak had noticed that Tinker was gone, so he ran to see where she might be.

Yikes!!!

He didn't have to go far, as suddenly he saw Tinker running for her life out of the neighbor's garage. Zak saw the fear in her eyes as she bolted forward with her little legs churning up the grass as she ran for her own yard. Her short legs wouldn't be enough to stay ahead of the neighbor's two Springer Spaniels, as they appeared right behind her in a heated chase. She had discovered their dog food in the garage, and they didn't like that. Their size was easily twice that of Tinker, and they were gaining fast. Tinker was so afraid that she didn't even see Zak standing there. As she ran passed Zak he could tell the two larger dogs would soon catch Tinker. Thinking fast, Zak stepped on Tinker's long leash as she ran by. As the length of the leash ran out Tinker's forward motion came to a sudden stop. By then the two large dogs were racing so fast that they couldn't stop in time and angrily flew passed Tinker like two roaring racecars. Before they could reverse their course and come back Zak had scooped Tinker up and held her in his arms, then commanded the two dogs to go back home. Zak could feel Tinker's little heart racing as he held her. She was never so happy to be in his arms as at that moment, and showed it by kissing him all over his face. Needless to say Tinker never approached that garage again, even though she and the two Springer Spaniels became friends over time.

But a puppy's life sure can have some exciting moments.

Tinker's favorite things...

In Tinker's yard was a lovely little pond that was home to a beautiful Swan Betty named "Sweetheart." Tinker loved to lie on the pier and watch the swan as it swam in circles near her. During the summer she also learned to ride in Betty's paddlewheel boat.

To be able to get into the paddlewheel boat and float lazily on the water like the swan was a special treat. All Betty had to do was say, *"Tinker do you want to go for a boat ride?"* Tinker's ears would stand straight up, and as Betty headed for the pier she ran excitedly down the steep hill and onto the pier to wait for Betty to get there. Betty would then place her hand behind Tinker and Tinker would lower her "hinder" into Betty's hand so that Betty could pick her up and put her in the boat; then off they would go in search of Tinker's swan friend. Betty and Tinker loved doing things together.

At first Tinker didn't understand the pond. As a young puppy first exploring her new yard she ran excitedly down the hill to explore it. The pond had a ring of green algae around the shoreline that day that may have looked like grass to Tinker. She ran straight into the algae before she could stop. When she crawled out of the pond she was covered in green algae from head to toe. She ran back up to Betty with a surprised look on her face, not understanding just what had happened. Another lesson was learned, and she always approached the shoreline carefully after that.

Adventures were not always dangerous. Tinker became very fond of riding in Betty's wheelbarrow as Betty pushed it along from flowerbed to flowerbed tending her gardens.

"I'm queen of the garden," she thought, as she enjoyed hours walking through Betty's freshly weeded flower gardens sniffing out bunnies that she never was able to catch. She loved to chase them all the same, never tiring of the chase.

All business...

If it seems that all Tinker did was play, that wasn't the case. Zak had his office on the second floor of their house. The office windows went down almost to the floor, so Zak built a short riser and put Tinker's pillow on it so that Tinker could see outside. Tinker would spend hours each day with Zak and Betty as they worked in the office. She could see the front yard and the driveway, and carefully watched for any movement outside. *"I should promote her for being so dedicated to helping us,"* Zak said to Betty. At that moment Zak decided to make Tinker the vice president of shipping and receiving. She took her job very seriously. When the UPS truck approached she would sit up straight and watch it. If the truck turned into the driveway she would alert Zak and Betty by barking, and then she would run down to the door to greet the deliveryman. Tinker, Betty, and Zak became a great team.

Come on you two, it's bed time!

There is a time to go to bed...

Puppies know when they are tired. They can take a snooze anywhere, at any time of the day. But, as evening comes on Tinker wasn't interested in just lying on the floor. She loved the softness of the quilts on the bed, and snuggling up to Zak, so when her built-in puppy-clock told her it was time to go to bed she insisted that Zak and Betty come to bed as well. Every night at about the same time Zak and Betty would hear the jingling of Tinker's collar tags brushing against the railing in the upper office. There, with her head between the railing, Tinker stared down at Zak and Betty and *"Woofed."* They came to know what that meant. Tinker was telling them it was time to go to bed, and there was no use trying to change her mind.

Family...

Betty and Zak knew full well how much love Tinker added to their lives. They were family. When it came time to say farewell Tinker knew she couldn't have ever hoped to be loved more. After many happy years the little "Guardian Angel" silver tag on Tinker's collar was finally being called to duty. The fresh warm fields and sparkling ponds of puppy heaven awaited her as she went to sleep in Zak's arms. She knew they would all be together again some day. Until then, Betty knows she is sniffing and happily rolling in heaven's fresh clover with her tail forever wagging happily. Puppies are like that.

Sharing the real Tinker
with every little boy and girl

I've had fun telling you of some of the adventures that I shared with Tinker. I hope you have enjoyed her story.

Now I would like to show you some real photos of Tinker as we played together.

Tinker

The photo above is Tinker on her 12th birthday.

The picture on the cover of this book is Tinker when she first came to live with us as a puppy.

Tinker loved to play Hide and Seek with Betty while Betty tended her flower gardens.

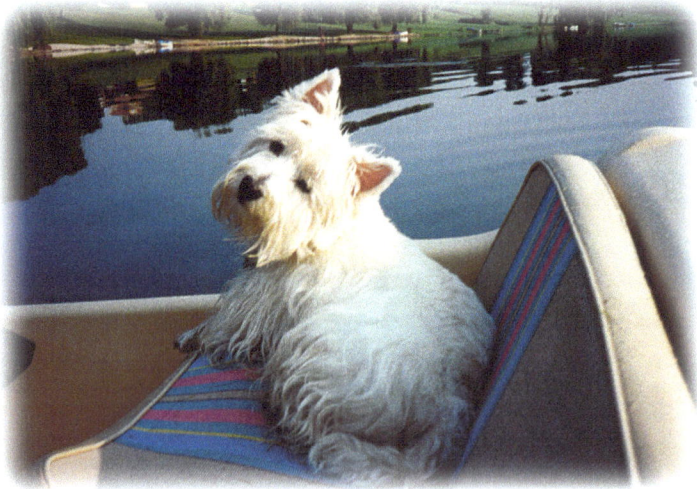

A restful day floating on the pond in the paddle-wheel boat with Betty was always a special time.

Playing was hard work for a puppy with short legs, but Tinker loved helping to feed her friend the swan and the wild ducks that made their home at the pond each summer. Then she would race Betty back up the hill for a treat.

After playing hard, just taking a lazy minute or two to lie on the deck in the warmth of the sun was a welcome reward.

Her red collar and silver tags can be seen around her neck.

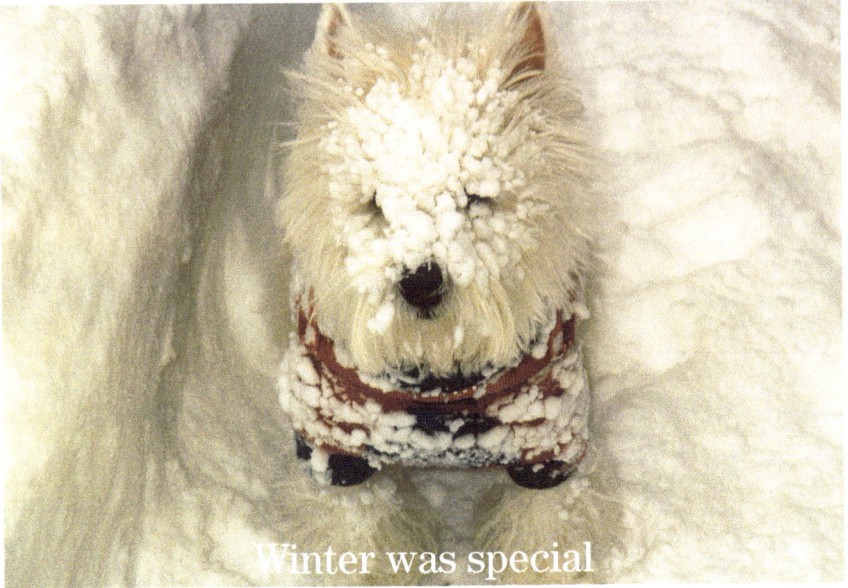
Winter was special

Once Tinker learned what snow was she wanted to play in it for hours. The photo above is Tinker's face full of snow after she buried her head in a snowdrift.

Her snowsuit kept her warm while she played.

After a hard day of playing outside Tinker loved to curl up and watch television with Betty on the couch, or just sitting on the floor.

With Zak it was different. When he picked her up in his arms she would bury her nose in his collar and slowly fall asleep.

But, on schedule, there was no mistaking when Tinker thought we should all go to bed. She would run upstairs and look down on us as she "woofed." It was her signal to say "bedtime."

Well that is Tinker's story boys and girls. She was always happy because she knew she was loved very much. If you have a puppy it will love you forever, so love it with all your heart.

Tinker's story is like every other puppy's story. Play with them, hug them, and love them. And when you grow up big and strong you will always remember them lovingly as I have.

I hope you have enjoyed meeting her.

As a special treat we invite all of the children that have enjoyed this true story to discover Tinker's voice as spoken by Caylee Birrittieri.

Smile and chuckle as Tinker expresses her puppy thoughts while experiencing the things in her life for the first time.

Simply go to **www.stonehedgebooks.com**
and click on the Tinker's Tale book.
It will take you to Tinker's page and the fun two minute video.

www.ingramcontent.com/pod-product-compliance
Lightning Source LLC
Chambersburg PA
CBHW041755050426
42443CB00023B/8